Piggybacked

Piggybacked
poems

Joanne S. Bodin

Piggybacked: poems
Copyright ©2011 Joanne S. Bodin

ISBN: 978-0-9827303-8-6
Publisher: Mercury HeartLink
Printed in the United States of America

Book design by Mercury HeartLink
Front cover: Splash Ink painting by Joanne S. Bodin
Interior: Splash Ink paintings by Joanne S. Bodin (digitally rendered from color to black and white by Stewart Warren, Mercury HeartLink)
Back cover portrait photography by: Peter Grahame, Ironic Horse Studio, Albuquerque, NM

All rights reserved. This book, or sections of this book, may not be reproduced or transmitted in any form without permission from the author.

Permission is granted to educators to create copies of individual poems for classroom or workshop assignments.

Mercury HeartLink
www.heartlink.com
editor@heartlink.com

Contents

Acknowledgments

About the Illustrations

Dedication

Introduction

Beginnings

    Thoughts from a Seven-Year Old   1
    Alone in the Asphalt Corner   2
    The Blood Test   4
    Winter is for Children and Dreamers   6
    A Girl of Four   7
    I Am From   8

Wedding Cake Hunger

    Wedding Cake Hunger   13
    Suburbia   14
    Birth   15
    Piggybacked   18
    Ode to My Muse   19
    Royal   20
    Twilight Child   22

Song for Twilight Child   23
Pacifier   24
Fish Tank   25
Taps   27
Beyond Innocence   31
Waiting   32
The Rainwalk   34
The Affair   35
I Offer You Winds   36

Night Dreams and Day Dreams

Rebirth   41
Animas   42
Anima   43
Train   44
The Seal   46
Halcyon   48
The Caller   49
The Chill   50
Yellow Dog   52
Minotaur of My Labyrinth   54
Helium Balloon   55
Spaces   56
Ode to Day   58
Phantom   59
Inception   60
Color Amber   63
Crescent City   65

The Journey

Parting   69
Fourth of July   70
I Wish   71
New Year   72
Venice Beach, Los Angeles   73
They Rainbow   74
Los Angeles Goodbye   75
Sedona   76
Santa Fe, New Mexico   78
Desert Winds   79
The Hawk   80
The Shadows Are Gone   81
My Spring   82

Love and Friendship

Women of Wisdom   87
Images of Love   88
Portrait of a Middle-Aged Woman   89
Princess Carmelita and Sir Lancelot   91
Reunion with an Old Friend   92
Moon Mom   94
Glow   95
Your Purple Dawn   96
Sister of Mercy   97
Vast Stillness   99
Gentle Quiet Ones   100

Child of the Islands   101
Black Sisters   103
The Bag Lady   105
Lady in Pink   106
Our May Garden   108
Ghost Ranch Mountain   109
The Clouds Tell All   110

From Distant Shores

From Distant Shores   115

Selected Poems by Samuel Bodin, translated from Yiddish by Sol Beckerman

My Love   118
My Step   119
Renewal   120
The Mirror   121
My Years and I   122
Sabbath Afternoon   123
People   124
A Sunny Dream   125
I Miss Something   126
To God   127
I Like To   128

About the Author

Acknowledgments

I wish to thank the following people for believing in me and for encouraging me to pursue my dreams: my two children Aaron and Stacy, who have always been the source of my inspiration; my ex-husband Stuart and his wife Irene, who have been my best fans; my brother Paul and his wife Peggy, for being my Rocks of Gibraltar; my grandfather, for his invincible creative spirit and poetic view of the world; my poet friends at UCLA, for their countless hours of inspiration; Southwest Writers of New Mexico, for their continued support, unlimited resources, and dedicated staff; Billy Brown, for his dedication to the poetry community in New Mexico; Stewart Warren, for his discerning eye, creative spirit, and editorial expertise; Ming Franz, for introducing me to the world of Splash Ink; and my best friend and partner Rona Fisher, for embarking on this journey with her unconditional love and encouragement

About the Illustrations

The technique of Splash Ink originated in China in the 8th Century in the Tang Dynasty. In contrast to the rigid discipline of traditional Chinese calligraphy and brush painting, Splash Ink allowed for much freer artistic expression with its large brush strokes and experiments with ink and color flow. In order to create a painting using Splash Ink, the artist uses up to five layers of **Ma** (mulberry) paper and pours black ink, along with other primary watercolors, creating an abstract image. After the sheets of Ma paper are completely dry, the artist separates them, and each sheet is hung on a wall or flat surface. The artist then views the abstract images of ink with watercolor and creates a painting based on what "calls out to them." They may see mountains with trees, spring cherry blossoms, waterfalls, oceans with jagged cliffs, fields of flowers, or wintry snow scenes...

The Splash Ink paintings in this book were done by the author at the New Mexico Art League. Her instructor was Ming Franz, author of **Splash Ink with Watercolor: Looking East Painting West.** www.mingfranzstudio.com.

The six Splash Ink paintings inside the book were originally in color and were digitally rendered in black and white by Stewart Warren, Mercury HeartLink. www.heartlink.com.

*In memory of my beloved parents,
Nate and Myrtle Bodin,
who gave me the courage and strength
to follow my muse.*

Introduction

My grandfather died at age ninety-five by starving himself until his withered body succumbed to pneumonia. I used to take my two children to visit him at Menorah Village in Reseda, California. We'd sit on lawn chairs under a huge Sycamore tree and I would play my lap dulcimer while my two children picked dandelions and made daisy-chains. Grandpa loved to talk about the "old country" and how he managed to escape from Russia as a stow-away on a ship to America; how my grandmother lost hearing in her left ear when a bullet exploded a few inches from her head during a Cossack raid in her village; and how his name was changed at Ellis Island from Budnisky to Bodin because the immigration officer couldn't pronounce the name in Russian.

    One rainy Sunday I ended up going to visit Grandpa alone. It was too cold to sit under the sycamore tree, so I sat with him in his room. I had put together a folder of a few poems that I had written for a class at UCLA to share with him when suddenly he blurted out, "Did you know that I write poetry, too?" He leaned over, reached for a stack of papers on the small table next to his chair and said, "They're in Yiddish. Do you understand Yiddish?" He knew I didn't understand Yiddish, but proceeded to thumb through the handwritten poems until he found one to read. First he read in Yiddish, then attempted to translate it into English. It was a love poem, perhaps for my grandmother who had died two years earlier, or perhaps to a secret lover from days gone by. And as he read each word, each phrase, each image, it felt like I was being transported to his homeland, to the fertile soil of his village near Kiev, and into the void of forgotten dreams. It was as if, for that brief moment in time, our souls had merged into one. We both saw the world through the same eyes—the eyes of the poet. After he died, I had the poems translated into English, and the more I read from his poetry the more I realized how we shared similar world views.

The day he died, the alarm clock went off at exactly 6:00 a.m., that is, the alarm clock in my daughter's room that we had purchased at a garage sale a few weeks before. But we had never been able to get the alarm to work. It was her first clock, as she was a first grader and needed to learn how to tell time. Later that day, I got a call from my mother saying that the hospital had called her to say he had died. Something prompted me to ask her what time. She paused and said, "A little before 6:00 a.m."

Was it coincidence or something else? We never got that damn clock to ring again. That eerie sound at six in the morning that jolted us out of sleep haunted me for years. Yet, in some strange way, it also served to inspire my own poetic view of the world. This book, a testament to the last thirty years after my grandfather's death, is a result of my own journey from distant shores. It is not as dramatic as his. I did not need to stow away on a ship from Russia. I did not see my family burned in ovens by the Cossacks, and I did not watch my people being slaughtered systematically, village to village, in my homeland. No, my journey was much gentler, more of a spiritual one. It was almost one-hundred years later, a different time in history. It emerged out of the New Age Movement when spiritual awakening peaked on the West Coast and when self-actualization became a buzz word. It came in a time when social change and political awareness did not topple the government, but rather served a small segment of the population who wanted to explore their own enlightenment. Yet, the driving force behind my journey was my poetic view of the world.

Perhaps my grandfather's poetry resulted from a different time in his life, when he no longer felt the only safe place to hide was under a lifeboat covered by a canvas tarp on a ship to America. Most of the poems in his collection were love poems, not poems of political unrest or personal angst. He seemed to be at peace, happy in his last years of life. The poems in my book, **Piggybacked,** represent a time in my life when, if I could have hidden under a lifeboat, I would have. It was a time when I began to realize I needed to find my "distant shore" in order to feel free. And so, through the generations our journeys piggyback on our ancestors', and on their ancestors' in the stories we tell to our children, and in the poetry we use in our lives.

Joanne S. Bodin

Beginnings

THOUGHTS FROM A SEVEN-YEAR OLD

Last night as I lay down to sleep
I pulled the blinds way above my sheet.
I looked at the stars way up so high
and the beam of light that filled the sky.
No birds or bees just plain dark blue,
and the little white stars that glowed like dew.

That night our neighbor's lights were still on.
It was twelve o'clock, five hours till dawn.
But since my head lay down so low
all I could see were the stars aglow.

Venice Beach, California 1951
(first poem)

Alone in the Asphalt Corner

Alone,
in the asphalt corner
between the handball court
and the hopscotch game,
I gaze upward in dreamy thought
of celestial castles
and hidden worlds...

    I merge with the clouds.

Alone,
in the school playground
where children's laughter
softly filters through my muffled ears,

    I merge with the clouds—

into whimsical animal forms,
a white rabbit, a turtle, a bear.

And even when the shapes do not conform
to my imagination
I linger,
until the tempestuous white vapors
consume me.

Only an occasional glance in my direction
from an unsuspecting child or teacher
could reveal
my tiny, hunched body, sitting

alone,
in the asphalt corner.

The Blood Test

This day long dreaded,
nights haunted by sweats, nightmares.
Bland sweetness poured over my pancakes
or was it French toast?
Half-finished orange juice,
mother's downward glance,
"Do you need help with your shoes?"
White leather oxfords with
special supports to correct
a 3-year-old's pigeon toes.

Singing cryptic childhood chants with Father,
"Oh my darling, Clementine," to distract me.
He gets a new car today
after it's all over.

"Time to go, darling."
Coats secured, hats tied under chin
doors locked,
to the bus stop.

Familiar antiseptic smell stings my nose.
Rambling sterile walls punctuated by doors
and a drinking fountain.

Closer...
        Closer...
                Don't be afraid...

White-robed doctors and friendly nurses say,

"Turn here, sit down on this chair."
Silver blade, so sharp,
unwrapped from its sterile package.
Now my finger
already throbbing with pain at the dreaded

PRICK!

"It's all over now. Good girl.
You're so brave. Have a lollipop."

Winter is for Children and Dreamers

Slosh through puddles and gutters
letting cold rainwater seep through
lambswool socks
feeling each squishy step.

Stomp on moldy maple leaves
with wet galoshes,
smell a forest of sweet sap
dripping on virgin snow.

Fondle an icicle on a willow branch.
Bend over to suck around
the glistening cylinder
yet do not break it off—
as a souvenir.

Winter is for children and dreamers,
oatmeal cookies and hot cocoa,
a raging fireplace with
the scent of cedar,
and Father in the rocker
smoking his pipe.

A Girl of Four

A girl of four squinting
into the sun-soaked morning,
holding a toy windmill fluttering
in the breeze.

The magic eye of her daddy's camera lens,
captures the gentleness of that day—
into reels of memories.
She waves innocently into the movie camera,
wears the purple pinafore made by her mother.

Did her parents guarantee a free passage
into her fairy tale world
where gentle breezes rock her to sleep?

Could they really protect her
from giants,
and wizards,
and power?

I Am From

I am from a place near the ocean
where fog horns warn of
approaching planes.

I am from perfumed rose gardens
and backyards filled with
fruit trees—
lemon, peach, apricot, plum.

I am from treasure boxes buried
in backyard soil,
with hidden notes of teenage
blood-sister pacts.

I am from plaid taffeta skirts,
bobby socks and saddle shoes,
Father Knows Best,
and TV dinners.

I am from Mammoth Lakes,
crystal clear waters,
obsidian arrowheads
near Devil's Post Pile.

I am from the lower Mojave,
Hadley's Diner with date milk shakes,
an oasis of date palms.

I am from Joshua Tree National Monument,
heralding the coming of dawn.

Wedding Cake Hunger

Wedding Cake Hunger

A wedding cake hunger drives through me like a nail,
coating the years with iced stickiness
and indulgent bulges
so the numbness lasts long enough
between jabs—
sharp reminders of the two
sleek plastic figures atop the cake,
surrounded by love doves and wedding bells.
And of those green dollar bills
slipped quietly into my palm
from relieved relatives.

Now the moon, a yellow balloon,
takes me far away
on those nights, when the
wedding cake hunger consumes.
Then the moon and I disappear
behind the fluorescent shadows
of a new day.

Suburbia

Chalky visions,
hues of gray lateral boxes
filled with stiff forms
moving through hollow spaces.

Repeated paths twisting over and around
angular walls.

Fragile shell,
hollow shell,
yet sturdy enough for years of listless apathy.

Birth

I

Quivering muscle
uncertain how and when to begin,
waiting for those
tiny granules of hormone
to silently slip down rubber tubing.
Three days and nights
with false contractions,
confusing my body
now at the mercy of
a bottle of medical magic.
Looking up toward the shiny
sterile ceiling, I wait,
knowing in only a few more
seconds the liquid will arrive.

II

Darkness tunnels into my vision.
Timed by the clock,
every two minutes,
an eternity of contracted muscle
grasping, twisting.
Fixed gaze on a light switch
for full concentration.

Pant blow...
        pant blow...

breaths of cerebral control.
Weeks of Lamaze classes—
practicing, stretching and strengthening,
breathing and concentration.
Fathers-to-be with their swollen women.
Dr. Lamaze revered.
No turning back,
deeper, sinking.
Only seconds between contractions to turn my head
and offer a weak smile to my husband.

Pant blow...
        pant blow...
Focus.
Intense knife-sharp pain.
Bones give way to minutes ticking eternities.
Nurses and doctors waltzing
in and out of my body.
Offers of more magical powers—
a pill,
quick to throw my mind deeper into
confused concentration.
Blurred memories give way to
relief in temporary madness.
Obscure refrains of childhood songs
slur from my pain-drunk lips.

III

Sudden awareness.
Thirty timeless hours turn to an uncontrollable urge to

Push!

      Push!

Opening outward through darkened passages,
toward white sterile walls,
toward human hands,
toward father's urging gaze.

Closer,
      Closer!

Bursting, stretching, tearing,
twisting down channels of unknowns—
life emerges wailing.
A slippery mass,
yellowish,
purpler,
pinker,
a baby,
a boy,
our son.

Piggybacked

Masking their cracked undersides
they form a luscious cover,
new sprouts piggybacking their ancestors—
a cluster of leafy tradition.

At the top one leaf juts out alone,
basking in full sunlight,
no offspring to shadow
that fragment of precious time,
before it's piggybacked too.

Scientific name: Tolmiea Menziesii

The most unusual feature of the Piggyback plant is its means of vegetative reproduction. Adventitious buds develop at the base of each leaf's blade. From these buds, new plantlets develop, "piggyback" style, on the mother leaf. The result is a colony of plants developing from even one individual.

Taken from an Internet article, "Plant of the Week," Dr. T. Ombrello, UCC Biology Department

Ode to My Muse

Poor old dog,
cod-liver oiled and vitamin-breath,
my assuagement for that now
occasional stroke of affection.
Snails secretly creep into my garden
shearing fresh carrot tops to the ground,
leaving their nibbles on baby radish leaves
and shiny paths to the ivy.

"Snairol is fatal if swallowed
by dogs and children
use with caution."

The baby crawls freely,
spider-walking across the lawn
to the lemon tree.
Lemon juice dribbling from his innocent mouth—
allergic to citrus since age four months.
Baby cream doesn't help the burning raw rash,
the diarrhea, the seven diaper changes
or trips to the bathroom to empty my bladder,
sharing its limited space with someone new.

Oh, blend into my morning nausea,
the orange slices and soda crackers,
the dog shit on the carpet,
my blurry eyelids,
and lift me out
of this slot—
for an eternal moment.

Royal

I am royal, Queen Mother.
Queen of palatial household.
Queen of three balanced meals a day.
Queen of five hours sleep a night.
Ruler supreme of providing a stimulating
environment for an active toddler and
a curious newborn.
Of driving the royal carriage
to the marketplace.
Of choosing the most natural,
nutritious foods for their royal diet—
and of remembering to buy only special
foods for His Majesty's low-cholesterol diet.

I am royal timekeeper.
Queen of all the chores done before
His Royal Highness comes home,
so it looks like the royal palace glistened
and glittered that way all day,
in anticipation of his return.

I am Queen of runny noses,
and aspirin, and of fear.
Will the fever break tonight?
Should we let our friend's brat visit
so soon after the weeks of illness and relapses?

I am Queen of the royal bed,
between dreams and nightmares,
embraces and blurry-eyed kisses.

Queen of the royal hound and his nightly escapades.

I am royalty for sure.
I am reminded every hour of every day
of my importance,
my heroic pivot atop the throne of survival.
Yet you sneer when my gown wrinkles
or drags from misuse.
You shrug at my small talk
of the day's events.
You act surprised that my throne excludes you
so much of the time. What did you expect—
a nightingale in a gilded cage?

Twilight Child

You've found your hands today
and you delight, examining each pudgy knuckle
like a jeweler fondling diamonds.

You were named for her.
Arthritis claimed her hands, now gnarled and wrinkled.
Her mother's mother raped by Tartars
and your eyes, slanted sienna,
hold our shame, your innocence.

You can see your hands today.
She can see her soul.

Song for Twilight Child

Little one, twilight child,
your slumber is safe from the cold.
Your mother's home like she's always been,
only now she is feeling alone.

Precious one, twilight child,
your womanhood surely to come,
will show you the paths of fairies and saints,
and maybe yours won't be alone.

Little one, twilight child,
you see me the way that I am,
passing this time as your mother and friend,
but having the urges to roam.

Pacifier

It's only a rubbery substitute
and you intuitively know the difference,
but soon it begins to mold
to the shape of your mouth,
and soften against your tiny teeth,
and taste of your peanut-buttered breath.

You let it protect you
against their disapproving frowns.
You especially like it when you sleep,
to ward off night creatures,
and memories of your traumatic birth,
when you couldn't suck on a real nipple.

Some say it's because of that "thing,"
that you don't talk yet.
Some blame it on your being so shy,
while you quietly sit in a corner
rocking, and stroking,
watching your daddy smoking.

Fish Tank

Fish linger in the sunlight
like leaves outlined by threads of iridescence—
floating through a collage of watery shadows.
Each shape, a child's treasure
that he tries to snatch up
and store in his imagination.

I wonder what he thinks when
he sees into their watery world?
His fourteen months of life
have given him no clues yet
that their shadowy shapes are even alive,
or that he can't take his hand, and
run his fingertips along their shiny surfaces.

Except that,
as he presses his nose and lips to the glass,
he hears a loud "No" and begins to cry.
Like the slow rhythmic
sleepy nod of his head,
the fish swim back and forth
in their own dreamlike trance,
in mysterious circular precision.

And his tiny body begins to relax
as he watches, with tears
still dripping from his eyes.
I wonder what he thinks when he sees
their underwater carousel
interrupted suddenly,

when one fish darts out of pattern
to attack another fish,
and pieces of
skin and bone
emerge out of the chaos,
to float away,
to be eaten by one of the
synchronized swimmers
who managed to stay
in his own territory?

I wonder if he knows
that in this underwater metal tank
nature's laws of the survival of the fittest apply.
A diver descends, wearing a black wetsuit
and metal mask, carrying a
bucket of food and a microphone.
He feeds the fish
and in booming voice calls out their names.

They swim up to snatch their already dead relatives,
just thawed from the deep freeze.
I wonder if he thinks the diver is a fish too?
And when he grows up,
will the mysterious dream-like regalia
of the fish tank disappear,
when he is able to read
the overhead description of the
Lung Fish, who,
"only moves every six or seven months
to deposit a muddy turd."

Taps

I

Today the sun peers unashamed
into our backyard,
drying up mud-filled, rain-soaked cracks
overgrown with weeds,
waiting for our gardener's shears.
Today could be the first day of spring,
except for the notorious groundhog's hibernation,
reminding us of weatherman's warnings
for a longer winter.

I lie on my Thrifty's chaise-lounge,
soak up a few minutes of sun
before the baby wakes
for his three o'clock medicine.
Next door, through the chain-link fence,
a neighbor turns wet soil
around each rosebush—
pulls out winter's overgrowth of crabgrass
that managed to creep through
the brick-lined divider.
She vacantly looks at her husband's
middle-age body,
occasionally throwing him a sarcastic
remark about how
their 15-year-old, half-blind,
deaf basset hound "goosed" her
while she sat on the wet lawn,
and why didn't he sometime?

It was all the poor dog could
do to know the difference
between her smell
and the spot he last
buried his bone.

Each spring roses bloom
in their yard,
encircling their green
velvety lawn with
blinding colors
of perfumed perfection.
Unless a neighbor or friend knew them,
or overheard through the fence,
no one would ever know about their
27-year-old son,
who committed suicide
after three years of therapy,
at one-hundred dollars an hour.
The therapist was an old family friend.

II

Over the brick wall in the back,
a shrill voice yells,
"For the third time, Herbert,
take out that trash."
No answer,
just the sound of scissors
crisply snipping at his roses.
Next to his roses, he loved
carnations best.
The peppermint smell

reminded him of his
grandmother's store,
when people took carriages
to town to shop.
"Herbert, for the fourth time..."

III

Down the block,
Ben is selling his house
after four heart attacks in the
past year. His heart won't last
much longer.
Used up all his money
on doctors and hospitals,
and oxygen machines,
so might as well sell.
On sunny days
Ben sits alone,
in front of his freshly painted,
newly carpeted,
marketable house.

Walking the baby,
I stop and ask Ben how
he's doing.
Slow, slurred speech,
each time the same answer.
"As good as can be expected."
Except that today,
looking across the street,
Ben's chair is empty,
while the sun shines shamelessly

on Ben's spot on the porch.

IV

I cannot see our other
neighbors very well.
They mostly stay indoors
or work all day,
or peer out of their windows
when I walk the dog
to yell, "Not on my lawn!"

Since there is another
house for sale,
making five in the last month,
the remaining old timers
watch silently,
while their neighborhood changes
in the name of progress—
bringing in unfamiliar faces
only to be glared at
from locked doors,
and shaded windows.

The baby woke up. It must
be three o'clock.

Beyond Innocence

A moon flake drifted down,
settled on your brow,
and melted into your mind.
You bear the mark of her lunacy,
sanctified by her power and wisdom,
yet stifled by a melancholy scream.

Shadowed by your crescent longings,
you must reclaim your
birthright, Taurus—
and when lovers meet,
and oceans swell,
and wolves howl skyward,
your moon flake will shine forth
in prophetic splendor,
in spite of your
smug sneer.

Waiting

Foggy sky,
withered rose petals hang listlessly,
still clutching the apple-like core
waiting to fall,
to blend with the crabgrass
and mulch below.

Waiting, for the sound of
mechanical wheels
grinding the day to a halt
with the squeak of old brakes.

Waiting, for the fat to come to the top,
while the aroma of chicken soup
mounts with each bursting boiling bubble.
A sip of wine
from one of our fine Venetian glasses,
still fragile from the costly trip across
the ocean for our honeymoon.

A Beethoven symphony throbs
over wires from the
four-hundred-ninety five dollar stereo,
sale item speakers.
Brown eyes of a babe
exploring each new room,
conquering his strange new world.

New evening gown,
lace and red velvet,

covers my tired body,
waiting—for you
to smell the rose,
       to share the evening meal,
to see your son again,
       to love your home,
to know of my presence.

The Rainwalk

Street-lamped shadows glisten.
Puddles of twilight
linger along the
cracked pavement
to my doorstep.

The rainwalk beckons you,
to follow its watery glow
to the warmth of my
embered hearth inside.

The Affair

You caress her hair
you kiss her lips,
her scent envelops yours.
And at 6:00 a.m.
you meander home
to a quiet guilt,
a baby's cry,
the stench of a diaper pail,
the salty tears of your woman—
and an all-consuming fatigue
overtakes you.

You're sinking...
                sinking...
                              into blissful inertia.

I Offer You Winds

Do you love her, too?
Does she fill your thoughts
with memories,
and pain,
and reverence?

Does she still matter, so far away,
when a new cargo awaits you—
with mango and papaya,
caravans of gypsies,
spider's milk,
and winds?

Yes,
I offer you winds....

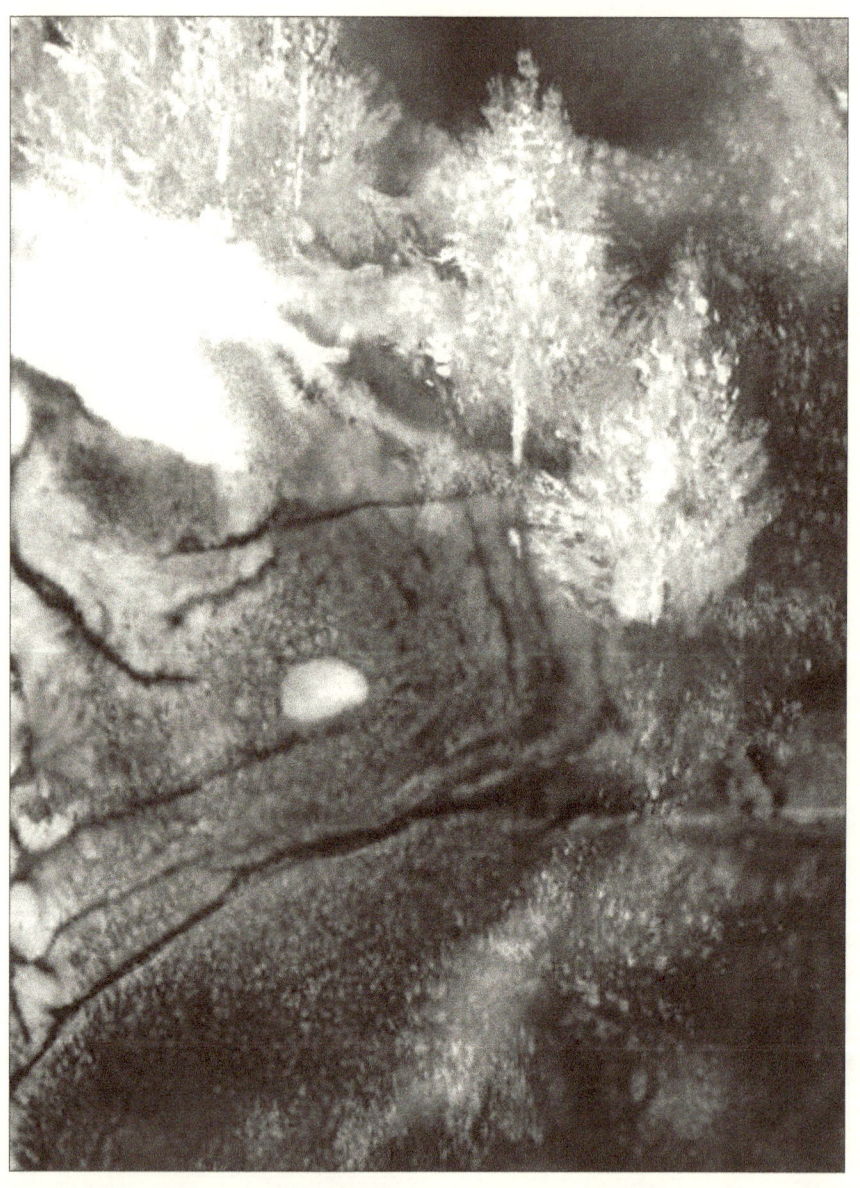

Night Dreams and Day Dreams

Rebirth

Her room—
light waxy blue shadows,
the new cradle rocking back and forth,
erratically.
She shivers from the cold.
Sudden spasms
rack her tiny body.
Her eyes close.
I fondle her little foot
and she peers at me
from the dresser mirror,
wearing a torn kimono.

Her scent of lavender beckons.
The wooden cradle squeaks,
turns to splintery coffin slats.
Struggling inside,
the tiny body gasps.
I see into her eyes
and suddenly feel,
a familiar twinge.

Animas

The armadillo appeared,
thick-skinned,
hunched.
I disturbed his resting place,
his bed of nocturnal dust.
He had concealed himself in my cellar.

When he appeared again
he stood erect,
arms stretched out
a butterfly of lacy cobwebbed ash.
Compelled to touch,
we stood at the altar together.
Creature of my cellar,
how can I learn to love you?

Anima

In white organdy, she enters.
Purple sage scents
her golden ringlets.
She says she loves spring.
I follow her far away
over rickety docks,
and oceans.
Her sweet liquors fill my mouth.
I smell her incense
and taste her freedom.
A slow drone at first,
a distant roar of wind
through pine boughs,
a wailing sitar,
a cry, jolts my consciousness.
I must return...

Train

I was on that train again.
This time the destination was—
unknown.
Babies, on my lap
hotel room warm, cozy
maybe a New England cottage.

Left the kids in the room asleep,
with a babysitter, and
went downstairs
in my Paris original dress
from Andorra.
Sat at the bar
and waited.
Two men walked toward me.
Our eyes met.
No words were spoken.
We sipped hot apple cider,
our past, erased with that one
glance of—
freedom.

Bar room glowed in muted light,
younger man asked me to—
fuck.
I told him I'd
go up to his room and
he was surprised.
I told him how
I'd died many times,

to make this moment
possible.
And, apparently,
so had he.

The Seal

I

One day I stood on the beach—
alone.
A giant seal, brown and furry
crept out of the icy water.
Our eyes met.
Our fear mingled,
and our strangeness kept us
comfortably apart
in our snug spots on the sand.

We stared at each other
then, with similar gestures
threw back our heads
to soak up the morning sun.

II

They are waiting for me—
fanfare of shark teeth
yawning their way
through icy waters,
sleek sailors
of decadent living
out for their Sunday regalia.

But they can wait.
I must first dig in wet sand,

run up to the break-water to caress
the barnacles—
pop seaweed balloons.

Halcyon

Still as the calm before
the great hurricane,
motionless tears begin
to drip down my face.
Time is a capsule
I swallow in writhing pain,
to sooth my mind with Anacin
memories of you,
sitting beside me here,
on our wooden porch,
gazing into my
sorrowful eyes,
while I
wait—
knowing you'll leave, this time
with the summer's scorch.
Rustles of spring
are watching
for darkening hues.

The Caller

I enter the black door.
Terror reveals his presence.
Mannequin stiffness,
black tuxedo,
waxen gaze.
He lets me scream against
the misty dust
of decaying pillars, and
centuries of rubble.

I have to get away.
I don't belong there
yet, the two workmen
restoring the altar
offer a smile—
and the sweet smell of
human sweat.

The Chill

I

I sit here
in the sun,
gaze out on
glittering oceans,
on steamy sand,
sweating with relief
for a few moments
of sun-soaked solitude.

A chill creeps over me—
warns of the coming
icy October blast,
even as I sit here in the sun.

II

My father lay
face down in the snow,
a woolen scarf
pillowed under his neck.
I try to pull him to the top
of our mountain
but he is lame,
so I leave him with his
half-grin of resignation,
and I slide down, down
to the trees,

to the people,
to the cozy lodge.

But today the sun's warmth
cannot take away
that chill,
that comes over me,
every once in awhile.

Yellow Dog

Today he's a yellow dog—
black squinty eyes,
a wrinkled jowl,
and a sneer. He lurks
in the upper left corner
of my mind, taking up
too much space.

I close my eyes and
he lurches forward,
cobwebs the darkness and
tangles my thoughts. He
stabs me with his smile
and self-satisfied chuckle.

The day he revealed himself,
I embraced him in fear.
Yet he struggled to be rid
of my desire. I am
learning his manner,
his habits,
when he can be caught
off-guard. We toss
our pain around and he
usually wins. I open
my eyes to let the sunlight
fade him back to his
corner, for awhile.

Today he's a yellow dog.

He used to be a werewolf. I wonder
if he'll ever be a flower?

Minotaur of My Labyrinth

You devour me
inch by inch, your
thick bull tongue,
your clenched teeth,
throbbing for my maidenhood.

Your opaque hollow eyes
gaze into mine—
sienna.
Your body, that of a man,
virile,
thrusting.

Can I satisfy you this time?
Must I surrender
before I can weave my golden thread
through our labyrinthine world?
I say "yes" to the minotaur.

Helium Balloon

Special assignment,
mission empyrean.
Others have already tried,
now it's my turn—
to float on centuries
of saltine waters,
to pull with earthly force against the
wrinkled nipple
of your silver membranous
cosmic mass,
hissing poisonous gases,
hovering above me with
magnetic closeness—
waiting.

Others have already died while forcing
their mortal will,
on your gigantic globular specter.

Spaces

Lumps of shapes all around.
Lumps surrounding lumps,
rounded,
moving gently,
unevenly.
Fixed, hard, shiny shapes,
reflecting rays of color
darkened by density.

White open lacy shapes,
criss-crossed and brittle.
Somehow I'm drawn to the
criss-crossed
brittle, unpredictable shapes,
not the familiar lumps.

I usually don't see
the spaces
between the shapes—
those invisible ghostly breezes
you try to avoid with cups of
hot chocolate and marshmallows.
But those spaces beckon.

I look at them for the first time.
Confused at first, I
pretend to see,
then slowly
they take form,
wrap around me in a blanket

of protection
of familiar warmth,
a womb for me to lie in
and rest for awhile.

Ode to Day

Succulent caresses,
banana-fingered moist breeze
spreading over
flesh-scented mounds of
eucalyptus-oiled earth.

Spider-webbed morning,
you entangle me with
sweet sticky windows of air.

Phantom

Phantom in black,
he sways to the right,
thrusts his leather-handled weapon.
His synchronized eyes peer
above his mug of frothy beer.

Confident,
he bends over the counter
to ask me for my phone number,
revealing a cigarette-smoked
reality through his phantom lips.

Inception

It's a tiny drop of dew on
a blade of grass after a rainstorm,
that won't let you shift your focus
until it burrows into your subconscious,
with tangled images that call out to you.

Then it disappears
for awhile.

But you know it's still there,
the melancholy thoughts
still disjointed,
pulling at you to give them life,
to tell their story,
until they weigh you down with abandon.

You try to convince yourself that
it's not your story.
You aren't even sure what they want.
But then the tidal wave,
no longer a tiny drop of dew,
the water envelops your subconscious
and debris of human suffering washes along
the shore of your mind,
and interrupts your every day routine.

Then it disappears
for awhile.

Until you are sitting at the Sixth Street Cafe

with your writing pad, pen
cup of Moroccan dark roast coffee.
The sound of rain pellets on the picture window
in the corner of your wooden booth.
The drone of a train whistle tunnels
into your subconscious.

Synapses begin firing away.
A train roars by.
Rain mixed with snow blurs your vision.
You look out of the window,
see the ghostly shadow of the red caboose as it
disappears into the mist.

Suddenly the fog lifts.
You see distant sun drenched fields
of poppies and columbine.
The entire story now unfolds
and you know everyone so well—
their stature,
their favorite foods,
their deepest secrets,
and your hand begins to write.

You dribble words onto
paper like creamy butterscotch candy
in metaphors of longing,
of pain and euphoria.
And they dance with you in a tango of sentences.

Floodgates opened, you stay with them till the
finish, not to win the race
but to honor their presence,

and the heaviness lifts.
Your muse gives you a creative wink
and runs off, to romp in her fields of glory.

Color Amber

I am amber,
the blood of the ages,
of huge redwoods,
of ancient civilizations.
I flow through eons of time,
through life itself.
Yet I elude even the most experienced
color connoisseur.

I am an amber vase,
atop an antique hutch.
Next to me, another glass bottle—
green.
I seem to be the focal point
on this hutch. My shimmer pales
green's opaque darkness, and
my round shape contains mysteries,
stories, literature beyond color.

Now I sit on your ring finger,
a huge rock of amber
encased in a sterling band.
Your favorite ring, you say.
Do you know that I really came from deep
in the Baltic Sea,
drifted over the centuries,
was plucked up by an amateur archaeologist,
formed into a shape,
sold to a jeweler in Santa Fe, New Mexico?

How lucky you are to wear me, near your heart.
You like my new shape.
I am formed to your specifications.
You say I give you good luck.
I remind you of your destiny,
your longevity,
your elusive muse.

Crescent City

Running from the wave,
that familiar foreboding roar
of water, of unleashed energy.
Tidal wave coming ashore
to devastate my little town of—
Crescent City,
along the west coast
of jagged cliffs, bluffs.

Meandering shoreline
that will be underwater in a flash
of my subconscious mind,
that wraps around this disaster,
repeated night after night in my dreams.

Jungian analysis helps
explain that the wave
is really my subconscious trying to be free,
from societal constraints,
that will one day
wash over my city.

Yet I never seem to drown
like you do.

The Journey

Parting

I paused.
My body shuddered,
but the wrinkles around my
eyes danced,
while sparrows gathered
worms for their babies.

Fourth of July

The world explodes,
in color falls of ethereal vapor,
celebrating my last July in the city.

The moon beckons.
Her light draws my naked body toward her.
I belong to her now,
among the trees and morning dew.

Those who know the moon
will find themselves, one day,
dancing among the rosebuds,
and stardust,
and light.

I Wish

I wish the trees had silver threads
to pull me far away,
from rotting roots,
and wormy bark.

Oh, Mother Earth,
your moist lunch of
soil-soaked mulch
is a medicine, a cure
I must endure,
to find my tree with its
silver strands.

New Year

Afraid to feel pain,
drops of rain on
my soul turn to icicles
piercing my resistance.

Remember the slow rocker
on hot summer evenings,
walks in the night
with croaking frogs,
and wild honeysuckle—
the un-rhyming melodies of the universe.

Venice Beach, Los Angeles

Boy do I feel weird,
in my Indian-linen laced blouse and
prewashed denims.
But he's wearing bells on his boots,
feathers in his belt, earrings in his ears,
and they're walking arm in arm
supporting each other's nervous twitches, and
aging bodies.

She's pregnant, with two little black faces
pulling at her skirt,
while she waddles barefoot.
And they're cleaning pigeon shit off the beach
so they can embrace.
And most of the others are alone—
or maybe with a dog,
and each one walks a resolute pace of
painful freedom.

They Rainbow

Through my dark glasses,
they rainbow fluffy wisps—
those clouds above our house,
above the boardwalk where I can't
even find a bench far enough away from
the smell of dog shit and garbage.

You said you hate it here,
in your pair of unwashed denims
with your crazy bitchy woman,
with your food stamps and reefers.
Then why do they rainbow fluffy wisps
above your house?

When we're alone, you rarely laugh.
You sit and study me.
Your gaze pierces my body.
Why do I sit here surrounded by
your Venice beach bums—
waiting, waiting
for something...
for the clouds to disappear?

Los Angeles Goodbye

I look at you through opaque eyes,
poisoned by your power and lies.
I waddle through mazes of stuff,
that makes me sing,
"I've had enough."

I see life now with eyes anew,
self-assured,
I'll see it through,
to find somewhere, a peaceful place—
a state of mind and open space.

I'm leaving dirty city streets,
and smog-filled malls of dying beats.
It's time to look inside my soul,
to find a way to live life full.
Be all the things I really am,
without the pretense and the sham.

I'm leaving dirty city streets
with memories of dying beats.

Sedona

I left a crystal in a cave,
in Sedona.
An exodus of sorts away from the city,
from my children,
a wandering into vast desert
to reclaim soul.

I left them with their father,
like the Quaker women used to do
when they had the "calling."
I nailed a mezuzah on their doorpost—
for protection.
I even buried a stone from the Rio Grande
under their porch,
a ritual in absurdum perhaps.

I cleansed my packed car with
burning sage in the middle of the night,
so the Orthodox Jewish neighbors wouldn't see,
to disapprove.
For how many mothers get to
leave their children to follow a vision,
a migrating instinct,
a soul journey out of madness.

I can hear children's voice now,
splashing, on Slide Rock in Oak Creek.
The clouds make eagle formations,
and I soar with them.
The crystal is my offering,

a return to its natural state—
in the dark moist walls of this cave.

Santa Fe, New Mexico

The earth turns red,
and your adobe houses glow
in uniform buckskin,
against the fiery sunset.

At seven thousand feet,
your thin air lifts my weary spirits.
I drift among the pine vapors,
and changing golden aspens.

They say you are a spiritual sanctuary
for healers, and eccentrics.
Yet I see your precious ancestors
huddled in woolen blankets,
selling turquoise jewelry
in your marketplace.

Desert Winds

You come through cracks and under the doors,
where nothing remains certain.
You rock our world with hot oceans of air,
 and grains of sand,
yet I sense a familiar warmth.

Today you comfort me,
with memories and reveries—
not like your chilling November brother,
who goes by so many names and guises—
who also, come to think of it,
has a familiar chill.

The Hawk

You soar high above the flattened desert plateau
and glide with gentle currents of air, sensing my presence.
You knew I'd come that morning to search for you—
so you play hide and seek with pure abandon,
swooping down behind a ridge of boulders,
then over fields of Joshua Trees standing like sentinels,
guardians of your desert.

When the wind picks up at a moment's notice,
and dusts your plateau with sandy memories—
you disappear behind a smoky cloud of obscurity,
and I know even you cannot stay aloft.

Now the walls rattle, and the winds howl lovers' wails,
and human cries of frailty,
and I shudder when—
a wail goes up for me.

The Shadows Are Gone

The shadows are gone, and everything looks
flat sandstone and inviting.
Sun paints the desert terrain with adobe peach,
and highlights Mother Rock,
as she smiles at her children of the valley.

I stand on sacred land hidden for centuries.
Her rocky landscape reveals her mysteries.
Even our ancestors could not escape the torment of their destiny,
and the secrets got lost again, and again—
buried into the modern age.

The night owl used to torment me
in caverns, with bats and dripping water.
But now the sun washes away my pain,
warms my skin, and offers a new beginning.
I am the morning of each new day, while
the night owl waits for someone else.

Lines around my reality grow vague,
as I fade into my dreams.
Did I come from your womb, Mother?
Or one windy morning did I appear,
out of this sandstone cave,
no tearing or twisting, or soft wet birth canal—
a free spirit out of the womb of earth.

I face the new dawn.
The shadows are gone.

My Spring

Drinking coffee in early morning—
my first day of spring.
Hyacinths, free from winter's hibernation,
undulate in breezes and dance with abandon.

Through years of wandering my vapid landscapes,
with newly-formed aging spots and thinning hair,
my spring now beckons me into uncharted territory,
always reminding me of the soft, moist earth
upon which I stand.

Love and Friendship

Women of Wisdom

It's up to us now, the women—
those last bastions of hope,
clay models of Mother Earth,
alive still, with shared visions.
No written word can help now.
It must all come from within.

The prancing buffalo gasps its last breath,
as the plains fire sweeps down to shroud its death.
We, of the modern age, hold ceremonial full moon rituals,
like our grandmother used to.
Menstrual cycles synchronized,
versions of puberty rites we bestow
on our confused teenagers, instead of sock hops and proms.

Undomesticated female energy fans the planet,
with cool breezes. A simple matter of the way it used to be,
when we celebrated life with the seasons,
and births,
and deaths—
but we still celebrated life.

Images of Love

In your arms,
I fade into an ocean of slithery
grey light—
entwined in our spiral dance,
belly to belly, our bodies
merge into the rhythms of drifting waves.

I see black seaweed against light shadows
prisming the darkness.
A cry pierces my bones.
Our eyes meet, and for a moment I'm
cuddled against your warm, fleecy body
looking out at our flock—
and the purple sage of the Pyrenees.

Portrait of a Middle-Aged Woman

You walk into the room,
purple flowers on cotton dress
above your knees,
with organdy sleeves.
You look fine.

Make casual conversation,
wait until the moment, when
you no longer feel conspicuous.
You fill space with
the day's chit-chat,
so you can disappear.

Your years show on your graying head.
Soft wisps of shoulder-length hair,
help hide your beauty- parlor past.
A school girl image does not really
conceal who you are. Your beads hang too low.

Weeping at the dinner table
over a childhood memory,
your thirteen years of therapy
don't seem to help. You say you feel raw, that
therapy has stripped layers of routine cover—
exposed you. What did you expect?

You seem vacant, in spite
of your outward garb of simplicity.
Now, you have only memories of nervous chatter
with your husband,

of stomach problems and doctor bills.
You swallow that pill, saying
these memories make you anxious.
Your heart pounds. You must get some sleep, so
you can make the 2-hour drive to the city,
for your beginners Spanish class.

Leaving the room, you still look fine,
except for the wrinkles on your
flowered dress,
and a few more around your eyes.
You were conspicuous in spite of yourself.
Maybe you should try blue jeans and work shirts.

Princess Carmelita and Sir Lancelot

You found me on the doorstep
of a dying way of life.
You told me that your garments showed
your pain and bore your strife.
Now I see you in the rainbows of my mind,
drifting farther out through years of endless time.

I saw you on your charger,
with your sword, a blaze of steel.
If I'd known you were a phantom,
I'd have forced myself to reel.
Yet you showed me all the things
I had to know.
Took me down those winding caverns
through my soul.
Maybe now, or soon,
I'll even let you go.

Then the twelve moons came,
and the seasons changed,
and the days turned into memories.
Now I stop in the tune
of a distant moon,
cock my head with a smile,
while I fade...

Into that folding darkness of our souls.
I glide across the heavens taking hold,
of that place, where all I see is brilliant gold.
And our music forms the distant shores of old.
Where a love like ours can shield us from the cold.

Reunion with an Old Friend

Talking to you—
not about your sheltered Mill Valley
organic-gardened cottage seclusion,
not about your crazy husband,
working as a line-man after his
nervous breakdown,
not those endless hours
devoted to issues, philosophies,
dreams, nightmares...

Talking to you—
not about my own loneliness,
roommate run-ins,
nights of insomnia.
Not about my repeated trips
to the med center, to be
poked and probed and told
it's only mono.

Talking to you again—
this time,
warm tinted curves of adobe walls,
my walls. Familiar black eyes of my baby,
staring into your wandering thoughts,
waiting for his dad to come home.

Six years have passed, and
our paths have crossed only this once.
You say your Mill Valley days ended?
You quit your job, traveled, never married again,

took four more years to recover
from a lovers' quarrel,
have no roots, no home.

Maybe you'll try Santa Barbara.
I hear it's beautiful there.

Moon Mom

Hot ginger baths,
incense burns spirals through
the steamy air.
Joni Mitchell sings—
blends into the night
with the owl's screech.

Jasmine tea leaves float,
toward the bottom
of the porcelain cup.
Night lurks around our adobe walls,
showering invisible moon beams
for our tomorrows.

Moon mom,
you fill me with satin pink
pillow fantasies.

Glow

I watch you in the glowing aspens,
child of light,
reaching into my soul—
like a necklace of silvery pearls,
unfolding the mysteries of life.

The heather turned cold today.
Snow clouds fill the heavens,
and you slowly fade into
the shimmering leaves.
Child of love, I embrace you—
and this moment in time...

Your Purple Dawn

The ocean rolls thunder,
on a horizontal glass slide—
while the January wind plays
rollercoaster games with seagulls.

I can see as far as Catalina today,
except for the rainbow sails
on the distant boat, blocking my view
of the cloud bank.

I know you are free now—
to ride across the waves on
a gust of wind,
to visit your tropical paradise,
to bask in sunny spaces between palm branches.

And when you think of us, still here—
gazing wide-eyed at our world
of the living,
I imagine that you might be sitting
here, beside me,
in your purple dawn.

Sister of Mercy

Sister of mercy—
pathfinder,
pioneer of courage,
soul sister,
midwife to those courageous few
who seek their destiny.

In the light,
like a moth to the flame,
I am drawn to your radiance—
yet this time my passion does not destroy itself,
in your fire.

The danger is not in the fire.
The danger is that mine must burn
as brightly,
or it will be consumed, if not by yours
then by the eternal cravings
of my soul.

Brook-melodies and water spirits sing
to me today,
as shadows of cattails ripple in
harmonic splendor.
Embers light up the hollow passages
of my body,
darkened from years of apathy.

Breezes whisper cryptic messages.
I find comfort in the music from

tall grass,
in silence,
in the still, small voice inside me,
in gusts of wind on the mountain top,
and in my detachment from the
hollow-eyed stares from the
people of the city.

Vast Stillness

I have wandered far away into the
vast, still, desert.
I rejoice at this new-found freedom,
soul-journey out of madness.
Then you come along.
You see shadows dancing,
and join in. My pain turns to ecstasy.

Your face between my swelling breasts,
the sweet nectar of mother's milk.
I am not being sucked dry this time.
Your hot breath between my thighs,
melts me into birthing splendor.
I am not being torn apart bone by bone.

I look into your ageless eyes, and see
Questa in the winter, with
snow-covered mountain peaks,
and feel alpine breezes against
my naked body.

Shadows become eagle-wings.
We soar above our madness,
making lazy circles above
cloud-covered sand dunes,
and dance in timeless wonder.

Gentle Quiet Ones

It's the gentle quiet ones who dance alone—
in frenzy,
and hide in closets, and light
ritual candles in prayer.

Her mother's favorite—
or at least the one who did what
she was told,
most of the time,
leading the family in prayer,
as her sister played
hooky, from church.

Then the burden became too much.
Her moments alone in the desert,
hiding in caves,
telling the truth to lizards
became her obsession.
If she's caught, she knows they will
hate her—
so she leaves,
stops in midstream, and paddles back
to shores of comfort and approval.

She just needs to remember those days,
when she knew the truth,
so nothing will stop her dance.

CHILD OF THE ISLANDS

Listen to the wind.
Listen to the voices
in the winds, child of the islands.
They speak from afar—
of worlds where light steers
star-ships and blows cryptic messages
of things to come.

Plant your ginger in deep brown soil,
child of the islands.
Dig deep.
Let the roots grab on to substance.
Let the white blossoms please you
with their sweet springtime scents.

Do you remember your roots
and what, of substance, they feed on
when the winds call you
to far off places?

Run through the sand,
child of the islands.
Let each tiny grain remind your tired feet
of their attachment to this earth—
of why you survived your years of pain,
of why you can see those prophetic wonders
of worlds to come.

Let the sand and wind comfort you,
child of the islands,

in these times of healing.
Hear the voices dancing around your body,
and smell the blooming ginger.

Black Sisters

Women of the shadow,
I look into your eyes, clear pools of sienna.
Centuries of your pain wash across my soul.
They told us to build our bubble-dream—
and fill it with wifely duties,
and two-car picket-fenced tombs
to keep us apart,
from each other—
from candle-light porcelain tubs
with daisy vases,
and Sunday afternoon soaks,
and lazy lovemaking,
and truth.

Black sisters,
when you look into each other's eyes—
your bond seals them out,
makes them wonder why you never go
to their office parties
or why Jay, the office gay, is your buddy.

Black sisters,
I wandered out into this desert
to seek truth. My bubble-dream burst, when
empty beer cans and dirty diapers popped it—
and I oozed out to fresh air,
and freedom,
and loneliness.

But now my tub is filled with hot ginger,

and the candle flickers brighter each day.
Black sisters,
thank you for sharing your shadows with me.

The Bag Lady

In the midst of a bustling city,
near the street fair, vendors sell
nuts, candy, and packages of dried fruit.
A bag lady walks unobtrusively, row by row,
shopping cart billowing with all of her
worldly possessions—
bread sticks, an ivy plant,
a suitcase, white plastic lawn chair,
a few clothes and blankets,
and a whisky bottle.

She looks directly into my eyes as if to say,
"Welcome to my world," then saunters off into anonymity.
A chill runs through me.
I know our souls have connected.

Lady in Pink

Parched landscapes meet up with the horizon.
I water withering cactus with a hose.
I might run out of water soon, but
cannot stop until it's done.

It's almost dusk.
Shadows creep along the desert floor
casting opaque hues over dry sand.
I stumble over small rocks.
Then the desert gives way and
darkness surrounds me.

I slip into the bowels of the abyss,
cling to the side of the cliff, holding on to the
rubber hose.
Suddenly, there's a tug on the hose.
Someone is trying to pull me up.

Rough sand, jagged rocks rub against my body
as I slowly ascend.
Setting sun casts salmon hues along the desert floor.
A hand reaches down, pulls me up the rest of the way.
I look up.

It is a lady in pink.
A maroon station wagon is parked behind her.
Pink leather heels cover her tiny feet.
A pink tailored silk suit covers her tiny body.
She sets me down gently, and
we both peer into the abyss and smile.

No words are spoken—
but I know I will see her again.

Bright moonlight washes over the desert,
revealing lush patches of desert wildflowers.
A gentle breeze brings the scent of freshly flowered sage,
and the lady in pink disappears in a mirage of muted dust.

Our May Garden

Summer breezes brush against
newly planted roses.
A shimmer of morning sunlight cascades
through our garden.
Last year's wild array of coreopsis,
morning glory, sweet peas,
no longer covers the rich New Mexico soil
in our garden—
for we have cleared out the clutter and disarray.

Well planned bouquets of roses fill our garden now.
Bouquets that never stop giving—in colors of
pearly pinks, luscious lavenders, iridescent yellows,
fiery oranges and snowy whites.

This May, perfume fills the air in our garden,
as the velvet red rose climbs to the top
of the vine, to signal a reminder of
our eternal love for each other.

Ghost Ranch Mountain

I sit in the shadow of Ghost Ranch Mountain.
The hummingbird flies to its nest.
Orange cream puff-like clouds
rise up from the valley,
as darkness descends; time to rest.

I wish you were with me, on Ghost Ranch Mountain—
your head snuggled deep in my lap.
Your eyes gazing outward
at Ghost Ranch Mountain,
so peaceful, no distance to map.

I left you to find my own
Ghost Ranch Mountain—
a place where the dolphins can sing,
and sunsets can ripple
a paint brush beauty,
where eagles can soar high on wing.

Perhaps you will join me, on
Ghost Ranch Mountain—
someday when you're older and free,
to sit in the shade with cottonwood blossoms
adrift with the wind in the trees.

The Clouds Tell All

The clouds tell it all.
Clouds reserved for special occasions,
when daylight pales in dreamlike luster.
Puffy and surreal, they hover above our
one-dimensional world,
and cast shadows against a dome of blue sky—
opaque hues of pastel that reflect dimmed visions
of things to come.

It was on one of those prophetic cloudy days,
that Mother took her last breath.
The apple blossoms were about to bud on the tree,
outside her window. Spring,
her favorite season, a good time to die.

I planted daffodils and pansies,
and filled the hummingbird feeder
in hopes of her yearly return to my garden—
the garden where her ashes lie,
the garden where she can come and go as she pleases.

The clouds tell it all.
Like cardboard cut-outs, the mountains stand against the horizon,
as if a gust of wind could knock them down.
Another prophetic cloudy day,
with trees barely budded, awaiting a new spring.
Perhaps she knew all along that you'd be with her soon.
You, her devoted baby brother.
You, with the fragile heart that finally stopped beating.

She takes your hand.
You play hopscotch on the sidewalk,
stop to smell the oleander.
She is your strength
you, her inspiration.
For the last time, you follow her along
the crooked road toward the light.
The clouds have spread out.
There is a clear opening of crystal blue sky.
She beckons, and your spirit swells toward the heavens.
You have both come home.

From Distant Shores

From Distant Shores

When the bullet whizzed past her left ear, then exploded,
they knew it was time to leave.
Blur of men on horses carrying rifles,
women carrying babies running, running from the Cossacks—
then the deafening explosion.
Samuel found her just in time,
blood dripping from her ear.

Stowaways on a ship from a far off land—
bodies cupped in podded space inside the lifeboat,
muted drone of waves crashing against the hull of the ship,
breath softened by darkness, to start a new life
in America.

They ran away from the city of their birth—
from fields of wheat,
from magical Russian winters and sleigh rides,
from their tiny village outside Kiev, where
they drank warm milk with honey,
ate fresh baked Challah steeped with melted butter.
But, they must make the ship before it leaves
for America.

There were others.
Rifka, the same age as Chava, only eighteen,
who sewed the family diamonds and jewels into her undergarments.
She would send for her family once she settled in America.
They all dreamed big dreams of a new world,
where they would be safe from the rifles, and the swords that
would interrupt their sleep, to stab at the fabric of their souls.

Ellis Island, port of entry—
the beginning of the rest of their lives,
and like the thousands of other immigrants, they found a
way to survive.
He became a paper-hanger.
She hid all his earnings beneath her mattress.

Said she didn't trust banks, refused to learn English.
Far from the distant shore of their native Russia,
they found what they were looking for, in America—
fraught with its own set of challenges, that millions
of immigrants had to endure, in order to be free.

Years later, they lay together again,
but this time there is no rocking motion to lull them to sleep,
no smell of salt water, or the stench of human despair.
Only the moist aroma of American soil, that holds the key to so many
stories of pain and suffering, of ingenuity and endurance...
of survival.

Selected Poems by Samuel Bodin
Translated from Yiddish by Sol Beckerman

My Love

Like tones hidden within silent strings,
so hold I love within my heart.
I wait for one to come and start to play—
Meanwhile, no one has appeared.

Over my heart soft spring-times have floated.
And suns drew out all the wine of flowers.
I opened all the windows and all the doors—
But no one ever came.

And always love remained unspoken,
buried beneath layers of harsh ordeals.
The earth cried out and agonized in pain—
And I no longer heard the voice of love.

Yet I know she flowers in me like everything that blooms.
Like all things beautiful granted by life.
And she will mature in my song, and ripen—
When it shall be easier to live on this earth.

My Step

I enroll myself into the golden years
and softer, more quiet is my step.
I don't know where time has passed me by.
I search for it in a song.

It is in songs I often find the nighttime hours,
as they extend in rhythmic beat.
I observe the custom of midnight study
as my grandfather used to do.
More hushed than mine was his step.

Let another song be formed here anew,
and cure and strengthen my step.
Shall I then present myself before God.

Renewal

The freshness of the dew,
The trembling of the leaf,
The secrets of the blue
which nourishes the heavens through.

The earliest twittering
of fledglings in the tree.
The first call of chiding
in rejuvenated heights—

Everything, everything proclaims,
"Soon the sun will rise on high."
And you tell me too,
"I'm coming! I'm coming! I'm coming!"

The Mirror

Always in the morning, whether summer or winter—
you meet your face in the mirror.
You notice how between the eye and temple,
grows a certain shadowy web—thin wings.
Regularly, every morning the mirror reveals to you
the head becoming greyer, greyer, greyer.
And in the thirsty pupils of your eyes—
Deeper, deeper, deeper, grows your sorrow.

Morning after morning becomes longer, longer, longer
Dragging on...more quiet and more restrained
You mark the silent smile on your lips
Now more depressing, twisted and out of shape.

It occurs to you to put your fist through the mirror.
But the heart takes fright and shudders, "You fool.
You'll meet your face in separate shapes
in every mirror splinter!"

A sea of sorrowful eyes looks out at you in pain.
You are left confused, perplexed.
Instead of the face you've been accustomed seeing
you're faced in great surprise, with hundreds.....hundreds.....

Joanne S. Bodin

My Years and I

I run after my years
In a wild gallop.
My years call after me,
"Go, you fool, run on."

I glance back at my years
In a silent stare.
Say my years to me,
"Don't back off, you fool."

I talk to my years
In a muffled speech.
Respond to me those years of mine,
"Weep not, wail not—laugh."

So I laugh at my years
And they laugh back at me.
Now we do feel and laugh again
At our luck of yesteryear.

Sabbath Afternoon

Every Sabbath after the meal
Come the neighbors to our home.
Young women in their wigs
And the older ones in bonnets.

Shyly, quietly,
Mothers and grandmothers.
They whisper it like a prayer,
"*Itenu*, a Good Sabbath to you."

My mother offers them a seat
And they take their places around.
On the table, large and open
Lies the Bible with its Yiddish style.

Jewesses of the Sabbath Day
In their bonnets and their wigs.
Straining ears for every sound
To hear legends of ancient lore.
Stories from the Yiddish Bible bound.
Words my mother would read and say.

People

I sing a song of the person
for whom gratitude has meaning and reason—
And who never will feel that he's lonely.

I'm annoyed to annoyance with those
who curse when they should be blessing—
Because with all they possess, they're still lacking.

I champion the concern of those people
who search and yearn for three to say Grace—
Yet this modest desire still eludes them.

I weep the cries of those people
who have too few blessings to count.
They have so little to be thankful for, because
whatever they had, has been ruined before.

I dream the dream of the person
who looks towards the day for his blessing
when, he'll have with what and with whom.

My walk is the walk of those people
who'll not shame one another.
But I have no feelings for people
who don't have it in them to bless,
nor any concern to condemn—
They are the lost and the wandering souls
who can't tell the difference between blessing and curse.
And their concepts of life aren't part of the world that I know.

A Sunny Dream

In front of my wintery window pane
Stands a tree observing the scene.
Little white feathers drop from above
The tree greets the first snow with love.

In front of my wondrous window aglow
The tree is dressed in a mantle of snow.
Little birds twitter to him from on high.
He responds playfully to their bright "Hello."

Before my wondering eyes
The tree dreams a sunny dream.
In his branches, hidden at the peak
Is a fulsome crown of stars in a stream.

I Miss Something

I miss something, always something missing—
Always I never have enough of TIME.
Perhaps it's because the world is small,
Or that its shores are far and tall.

Can it be that the day's too short
And the year is short of days?
No, for no miracle do I wait,
For much too long is my path.

My song have I long had in mind-
A forest grows, fields burst forth.
But some regrets I often bring,
When a song is short a note to sing.

To God

You brought me forth from your breast.
The stamp of Your I
impressed upon my being.
Like a child, I bent,
obedient like a horse—
In your way I went.
And anything you asked of me
I fulfilled as a decree.
I praised you, exalted you—
Yet you didn't quench my thirst.

In sleepless nights of painful emotion,
when my breast heaved with stormy confusion,
my prayers, beautiful and warm—
I sent forth to you, my God.
My weeping heart, through endless tears
prayed to you, my God.
But You, my God, did not accept my pleas.

I Like To

When I was a child,
It was with soap bubbles
That I liked to play.
When I was young,
I loved to chase after
Roosters and birds.
When I was older,
It was girls I liked to caress
and be close to them in green grass.

When I was a young man
I loved to ride horses,
and go sledding on snow-covered roads.
In my middle years
it was goodness I liked—
Gentleness, friendship
and to acquire and save.

When I reached my later years,
I liked to see myself in the mirror—
Clear and pure.
Now, no matter how old I become,
I like to think that my life
and my years, have not in emptiness
altogether been lost.

About the Author

Joanne Bodin, Ph.D., is an International Book Awards winner in gay/lesbian fiction for her novel, *Walking Fish*, which was also a USA Best Book Awards finalist, a New Mexico Book Awards winner, and a New Mexico Book Awards finalist in three other categories. Her current book, *Piggybacked*, is a collection of poetry that spans over forty years of her life and pays tribute to her late grandfather, also a poet. Some of his poems were translated from Yiddish to English and appear in this book. She plays jazz piano, is a watercolor artist, and is currently working on a novel about the esoteric world of orchids. She resides in Albuquerque, New Mexico and can be reached at 505/880-8326 or at jbodinauthor@gmail.com.

Her website at www.walkingfishnovel.com contains more information on her writing career. Both *Walking Fish* and *Piggybacked* are available at www.amazon.com.

www.ingramcontent.com/pod-product-compliance
Lightning Source LLC
Chambersburg PA
CBHW020906090426
42736CB00008B/509